WESTERN STEAM IN COLOUR 2

Hugh Ballantyne

First published 1990

ISBN 0 7110 1906 1

Published by

IAN ALLAN LTD

Terminal House Shepperton TW17 8AS
Telephone: Walton-on-Thames (0932) 228950
Fax: 0932 232366   Telex: 929806 IALLAN G
Registered Office: Terminal House Shepperton TW17 8AS
Phototypeset and Printed by Ian Allan Printing at their works at Coombelands in Runnymede, England

Cover:
Having just passed from Somerset into Devon whilst in Whiteball Tunnel, 'Castle' class No 7000 *Viscount Portal* picks up speed on the falling 1 in 115 gradient towards Burlescombe, and it's downhill all the way to Exeter St David's, with the southbound 'Devonian' restaurant car express from Bradford to Paignton on 17 June 1958. No 7000 was built in May 1946 and withdrawn in December 1963. *T. B. Owen*
Leica 111c 85mm Sonnar Kodachrome 8

Right:
Collett designed 0-4-2T No 1420 eases gently down past the Tiverton Junction distant signal towards the end of its journey on its return along the Culm Valley branch in East Devon with the 3.00pm mixed train from Hemyock on 21 June 1960. The branch was closed to passengers in September 1963 and milk traffic, once the mainstay of the line, ceased 10 years later in November 1973. No 1420 has enjoyed better fortune as following withdrawal in November 1964 it has remained in Devon at work on the Dart Valley Railway. *Peter W. Gray*
Agfa Super Silette Kodachrome 1 1/250, f2.5

Introduction

It is with great pleasure I am able to offer this second volume of historic colour pictures of Western Region steam taken in the 1950/60s. The original volume published by Jane's in 1983 was one of the first railway books published in England where a serious attempt was made at accurate reproduction of old colour transparencies to a high standard and for that reason the book was well received, so much so, that Ian Allan Ltd as successor to the Jane's series of colour books approached me for this second book.

Despite the technical limitation of photographic equipment and particularly colour film 30 or so years ago it is indeed fortunate that there was a small nucleus of competent photographers pioneering the way forward in colour photography. Readers today, when out enjoying the railway scene may find this a surprising statement when they see dozens, sometimes hundreds of photographers regularly recording virtually every interesting happening and certainly every steam special that runs anywhere in the United Kingdom. Thirty years ago it was quite different, the prevailing attitude was — even if you had the equipment and the money to travel frequently or long distances — that the scene would never change, steam would always be there. How wrong we were!

For this reason I hope you will savour and enjoy the wide variety of Great Western-designed engines, trains and locations to be found in the following pages, and give credit to my contributors, all individually acknowledged, who made the effort to obtain these now valuable and quite irreplaceable pictures of our railway history. For added interest and comparison with today's techniques I have, where possible, added known photographic details about the making of each picture.

To my contributors I extend my sincere thanks for allowing me to publish their work.

Hugh Ballantyne
Eccleshall
North Staffordshire
April 1990

Below:
Not long ex-works Collett Mogul No 7327 (see also page 51) heads south over Southern Region metals at Otterbourne, near Eastleigh, with a goods train from Washwood Heath, Birmingham, to Eastleigh on 24 May 1962.
A. Molyneaux
Periflex 3A f1.9 45mm Corfield Lumax Perutz C18 1/500, f3.5

2

The superb sight in the summer sunshine of an immaculately turned out Old Oak Common 'Castle' class engine. No 5035 *Coity Castle* sets out from Paddington on 27 August 1960 with the 3.10pm express to Wolverhampton, with the first of two stops only at Leamington Spa at 4.50pm and due at Wolverhampton Low Level station at 6.29pm. Such scenes of stylish and gleaming locomotives have over the years guaranteed a huge following for the Great Western Railway by its devotees and admirers. *R. C. Riley*

Agfa Super Silette f2 Sologon Kodachrome 8

Churchward type '45XX' class small 2-6-2T No 4565 busily drawing away from Coombe Junction to head south down the Looe River valley with the 10.05am train from Liskeard to Looe on 15 August 1959. The train has come down the 1 in 40 gradient of the track on the right from Liskeard into Coombe Junction Halt where the engine had to run round for the main 6¾ miles portion of its journey. No 4565, one of 75 of the earlier batch of light 2-6-2Ts, was constructed at Swindon in 1924 and withdrawn in 1961. Three sister engines of the class have been preserved and 11 of the later 4575 series also.
Peter W. Gray
Agfa Super Silette   Kodachrome 1

4

An interesting scene in the far west of GW territory at St Erth with two '45XX' class 2-6-2Ts making a pleasing symmetrical outline coupled bunker to bunker as they stable the stock of the down 'Cornish Riviera Express' in the down sidings on 30 July 1960. This train was the most prestigious on the line and departed from Paddington at 10.30am. It provided through coaches to St Ives which then had to be worked back up that short branch to St Erth for overnight parking prior to reforming next day as the up portion from St Ives. The locomotives involved here are Nos 4549 and 4570.
Peter W. Gray
Agfa Super Silette Kodachrome 1 1/250, f2

5

On the clear evening of 24 August 1962 a rather grubby 'King' class No 6016 *King Edward V* passes Solihull whilst working the 4.10pm from Paddington to Birkenhead express. *Michael Mensing Hasselblad 1000F f2.8 Tessar Ektachrome 1/1000, f3.5*

On the well maintained and rubbish free quadruple track main line east of Birmingham '81XX' class 2-6-2T No 8109 heads the 8.25am from Lapworth to Birmingham Snow Hill comprising a set of BR Mk 1 coaches on 27 June 1963. These large Prairie tanks comprised a class of 10 and were built in 1938/39 using frames of withdrawn '51XX' class 2-6-2Ts with new front ends, boilers with a higher pressure and coupled wheels 2in smaller at 5ft 6in diameter. This gave them improved acceleration on suburban services thus making them identical to the 70 locomotives in the '61XX' class. No 8109, contain- ing the frames off No 5133, went new in 1939 to Leamington shed and was the last to be withdrawn in June 1965. *Michael Mensing*
Voigtlander Bessa II Color-Heliar Ektachrome, 1/500, f5.6

A picture depicting the end of a short lived era at Swansea High Street station. On 8 September 1961, spotless Landore allocated 'Castle' class No 4090 *Dorchester Castle* waits to depart with the very last steam hauled up 'South Wales Pullman', the 4.30pm to Paddington. The last down train had arrived behind No 5048 *Earl of Devon* and the following Monday saw the introduction of the 'Blue Pullman' service, nothing less than the precursor of todays IC125 trains. No 4090 was built in 1925, became one of 66 of the class to be fitted with a double chimney in 1957 and was withdrawn in 1963. As a small point of interest this engine had a smokebox 4in longer than the rest of the double chimneyed loco-motives. *Hugh Ballantyne*

Voigtlander CLR f2.8 Skopar Agfa CT 18 1/60, f2.8

Certainly not GWR territory but the London & North Western Railway line which came into Swansea from Pontardulais and passed to Western Region jurisdiction following nationalisation, so it is appropriate that ex GWR locomotives should be seen there. Surrounded by the strong LNWR influence, seen in its signals, signalbox and station architecture, '57XX' class 0-6-0PT No 9677 draws out of Swansea Victoria station the stock which had arrived as the 11.45am train from Shrewsbury via the Central Wales line on 19 May 1964. This line was closed to all traffic in June 1964 and no trace of the station now remains. *Hugh Ballantyne Voigtlander CLR f2.8 Skopar Agfa CT18 1/125, f8*

A view at Welshpool on the Cambrian main line from Whitchurch to Aberystwyth looking east towards the peaks of the delightful Breidden Hills rising to upwards of 1,100ft on the English border. In a surprisingly quiet Welshpool station, Class 90XX 4-4-0 No 9027 stands at the down platform with a military special in July 1953. This engine was one of 29 hybrid locomotives rebuilt using 'Bulldog' frames and 'Duke' boilers and cabs which were commonly, but unofficially, called 'Dukedogs', which were used extensively on the Cambrian lines. Twenty three were rebuilt between 1936 and 1938 and the last six in 1939. They were originally numbered in the 32XX series and allocated names of Earls. The names attached to the first 13 were however shortlived, it being suggested that some peers of the Realm took a dim view of their titles being bestowed on such old fashioned looking locomotivies! With commendable commercial diplomacy the Great Western transferred the names to a batch of new 'Castles', numbers 5043 to 5055. In 1946 the whole class was renumbered in 90XX series in the same order as before. The engine seen here was rebuilt in June 1939 from 'Bulldog' No 3433 and 'Duke' No 3280 *Tregenna* and was withdrawn in August 1957. *J. M. Jarvis*
Kodak Retina 1 3.5 Ektar Kodachrome

The 'Manor' was a favourite class on the Cambrian section and a regular for this job about the time this picture on 1 June 1962 was taken of No 7823 *Hook Norton Manor* arriving at Machynlleth with the 11.10am Paddington to Aberystwyth, the down 'Cambrian Coast Express'. The 'Manors' used on the Cambrian at this time were generally kept well cleaned and the fine result is evident here. No 7823 was one of the 10 built by BR in 1950 and was withdrawn in June 1964. As a useful lightweight engine the class of 30 locomotives survived well towards the end of Western Region steam in 1965 and this has enabled no less than nine to be preserved, of which six have already been returned to service. *Peter A. Fry*
Kodak Retinette 1B Agfa CT18

Above:

Dulverton station was situated in a beautiful setting in the extreme west of Somerset near the village of Brushford some 2 miles from the market town it purported to serve. It was a busy intermediate station on the broad gauge line from Norton Fitzwarren to Barnstaple which opened in 1873, and gained further importance after the opening of the Exe Valley branch. In 1910 the platforms were lengthened, and the down platform at which '43XX' class 2-6-0 No 7304 is standing was converted into an island platform to give the Exe Valley trains their own platform. The Churchward Moguls allocated to Taunton shed put in a lot of work on this secondary line and in June 1963 No 7304 is about to leave with the 4.35pm from Taunton to Barnstaple Junction train whilst on the extreme right '14XX' class 0-4-2T No 1421 stands with the 5.30pm auto-train to Exeter St David's. *L. F. Folkard*
Agfa Silette Kodachrome I

Right:

A fine picture showing perfectly how a Great Western branch train blended into the landscape of Englands green and pleasant land. This is a view looking northeast across the valley of the River Exe to Thorverton station. 6¼ miles from Exeter St David's and the first station on the branch which ran from Stoke Canon to Morebath Junction on a line which provided a service between Exeter, Tiverton and Dulverton. The branch was opened in May 1885 and closed in October 1963 although occasional grain traffic along the siding visible behind the station to a mill continued until 1966. In this scene 0-6-0PT No 3659 is running into the down platform with the 3.20pm Bampton to Exeter St David's train on 8 June 1963. *Peter W. Gray*
Agfa Super Silette Kodachrome I

Running hard on the slight rising gradient through Sonning Cutting, a pair of two-cylinder 4-6-0s, with No 6809 *Burghclere Grange* (5ft 8in coupled wheels) piloting 'Modified Hall' No 7917 *North Aston Hall*, (6ft 0in wheels) race along the up fast track towards Paddington on 3 May 1958. None of the 80 'Grange' class engines survived to be preserved and No 6809 was withdrawn in 1963 whilst No 7917, built as recently as 1950 was gone after only 15 years of service in 1965. *T. B. Owen*
Leica IIIc 50mm Summitar Kodachrome 8

A very clean 'Grange' class 4-6-0 No 6843 *Poulton Grange* looks a most attractive sight making its way through Sonning Cutting on the up slow line hauling a class 4 goods train — one with at least a third of the train continuously braked — towards London on 27 May 1959. Mr Collett introduced these medium sized 4-6-0s to supersede the '43XX' class Moguls and were really only a smaller wheeled version of the 'Hall' class, the main visual difference being that the footplating over the cylinders was raised slightly. Eighty locomotives were constructed between 1936 and 1939 with this engine emerging from Swindon in October 1937 and withdrawn in February 1964. *T. B. Owen*
Leica 111c Kodachrome 8

The down 'Royal Duchy', 1.30pm from Paddington to Penzance, comprising a uniform set of chocolate and cream BR Mk 1 coaches, speeds through the Berkshire countryside west of Maidenhead near the village of White Waltham on the down fast line with 'Castle' class No 5034 *Corfe Castle* in charge on 2 July 1960.
T. B. Owen
Leica 111c 50mm Summitar
Kodachrome 8

On a crisp autumn day '28XX' class 2-8-0 No 2875 heads eastwards between Twyford and Maidenhead along the up slow line with a long goods train. This engine was one of a batch of 28 locomotives constructed in 1918/19 and the last of the Churchward series. Further construction as '2884' class under Mr Collett did not recommence for another 20 years. No 2875 was built in 1919 and withdrawn in 1964, being photographed here on 16 November 1963. It was a member of a class of highly successful goods engines which performed hard work well beyond the life expectancy for many locomotive types. *T. B. Owen*
Leica 111c 50mm Summitar Kodachrome 8

Perhaps the most impressive of all Mr Churchward's designs was his large boilered '47XX' class mixed traffic 2-8-0. The prototype was built in 1919 and eight more followed in 1922. They had a No 7 standard boiler and were fitted with 5ft 8in coupled wheels. Designed to work night express goods in later years they competently hauled both long distance fitted goods and in summer regularly worked express passenger trains between Paddington and South Devon. In this picture, taken on 13 September 1961, No 4705 is on an ex-works running in turn from Didcot back to Swindon and standing at Steventon station looks quite impeccable in its lined green livery. In front of the engine on the up side of the line can be seen the small Brunel timber goods shed. Steventon and all the other local stations between Didcot and Swindon were closed in December 1964. *R. C. Riley*
Agfa Super Silette f2 Sologon Kodachrome 8

A portrait of a beautiful and stylish Churchward locomotive. Mixed traffic Class 47XX 2-8-0 No 4705 stands in the autumn sunshine at Laira shed on 25 September 1960, Plymouth, coaled and ready for its next job. These engines were originally employed on night express goods between London, Wolverhampton and South Devon but in later days were concentrated at Old Oak Common and Bristol. They were at home on fast long distance goods or passenger trains save the fastest expresses but because of weight and length of wheelbase their availability was somewhat restricted. Unfortunately they were never named although it seems Mr Collett did propose they should be given old broad gauge engine names (how very appropriate) but this was not authorised. Even so, they still contrived to look supremely elegant in lined green livery, as seen here. The whole class was withdrawn between 1962 and 1964 and this engine went for scrap in December 1963, by which time it had covered 1.6 million miles, which was the highest mileage recorded by a member of the class. None of these locomotives was saved for preservation.

R. C. Riley

Agfa Super Silette f2 Sologon Kodachrome 8

On the Severn Valley line, then just a north Midlands secondary line in the GWR system, but now known nationally as a premier restored steam railway. '43XX' class 2-6-0 No 6393 comes round the curve southwards into Arley station with an up goods train to Kidderminster. The Severn Valley line was closed to passengers and goods north of Bewdley, in 1963 except for coal trains from Alveley which continued until 1969. Reopened in stages from 1970, the railway now enjoys an unprecedented popularity, so this picture has not passed completely into history, as one of the Collett series Moguls. No 9303 is under long term restoration and will eventually be seen in these same surroundings. 18 October 1953. *J. M. Jarvis Kodak Retina I 3.5 Ektar Kodachrome 8*

Another preserved railway, the West Somerset Railway, currently operates the bulk of the former Minehead branch between Bishops Lydeard and Minehead. Originally opened in 1862 it connected with the main line west of Taunton at Norton Fitzwarren Junction and this station, Crowcombe, just over 7 miles from Norton Fitzwarren is beautifully situated on the western slopes of the Quantock Hills. The station is at a line summit and had a long loop, which on 24 August 1963 '5101' class 2-6-2T No 4143 has just passed and is accelerating down the 1 in 81 gradient towards Taunton with the 2.20pm Minehead to Paddington through train, hence the engine displaying 'A' class express train lamps. BR closed the branch in January 1971 and it is to be hoped the present company will eventually reopen the remaining portion after securing BR agreement to allow trains to run to and from Taunton.

Peter W. Gray
Agfa Super Silette   Kodachrome 1

On the bright morning of 4 November 1960 a pristine ex-works '61XX' class 2-6-2T No 6106 has just arrived at Platform 5 at Bristol Temple Meads with the 7.15am local train from Swindon, via Badminton. This was a regular train used for running in ex-works locomotives, so could be relied on to produce a smart freshly painted locomotive, often from some distant shed. No 6106 was one of a series of 70 engines built between 1931 and 1935 and similar to the '5101' class save that their boiler pressure was set at 225lb/sq in against 200lb/sq in of the latter. They were specifically constructed to work accelerated London suburban services and they consistently remained in the London Division for over 20 years, only moving in later times. Thirty one of them survived until 1965, which was the final year of Western steam. This locomotive lasted right through until December of that year and had the good fortune to become the only survivor of the class being purchased by Mr D. M. Rouse and it is now kept at the Great Western Society depot at Didcot. *Russell Leitch*

The view inside Bristol St Phillips Marsh shed on 28 July 1963, looking across one of the two turntables in this roundhouse at a '57XX' class 0-6-0PT, 2-8-0T No 4265, 2-8-0 No 4701 and two 'Hall' class locomotives on the right. This important shed, coded SPM by the GWR and 82B by BR, housing mainly goods and shunting engines required in the district and at the end of 1947, it had an allocation of no less than 142 locomotives. It was built in 1910 and closed in June 1964. Following redevelopment of the site no trace of it now remains. *T. B. Owen*
Leica M2 50mm Summicron Kodachrome 1

On the South Wales direct line 'King' class No 6019 *King Henry V* has steam to spare as it sweeps effortlessly past Patchway station and starts the sharp descent into the Severn Tunnel with the down 'Red Dragon' — the 5.50pm Paddington to Carmarthen express — on 1 July 1961. It was only in the later years of Western Region steam that the 'Kings' were permitted on this route and even then they only went as far west as Cardiff. No 6019 was built in 1928, fitted with a double chimney in 1957 and withdrawn in September 1962. *T. B. Owen Leica M2 85mm Sonnar Kodachrome 1*

At one time there was a short loop line northwards from Severn Beach in South Gloucestershire which connected with the main line to the Severn Tunnel by trailing in from underneath that railway near Pilning High Level station. Most trains using this branch ran between Bristol Temple Meads and Severn Beach via Avonmouth, but six or seven per day would continue up the loop as seen here with a '57XX' class 0-6-0PT in September 1964 passing the location of the former Pilning Low Level halt as it climbs towards Pilning High Level with a train to Bristol Temple Meads. This service between Bristol and Severn Beach via Pilning was withdrawn on 23 November 1964. *Roy Hobbs*
Agfa Silette f2.8 Solinar Kodachrome II 1/60, f2.8

The Didcot Newbury & Southampton cross-country line once formed a useful link from the south Midlands to Hampshire. During World War 2 it saw an enormous amount of military traffic when it became of great strategic importance as a route from the north of England to south coast ports.

South of Didcot the railway climbed on a ruling gradient of 1 in 106 to the Berkshire Downs, an open expanse of beautiful downland country across which the ancient Ridgway, a pre-Roman roadway ran in parallel along the scarp of the downs. Churn was a remote little station serving isolated farms and

on 26 February 1960 0-6-0PT No 4649 makes its way towards Didcot with a local goods train.
T. B. Owen
Leica 111c 85mm Sonnar Kodachrome 1

Looking in the other direction to the picture opposite just north of Churn near the local line summit, '43XX' class 2-6-0 No 6313 is finishing its 6½ mile climb from Didcot East Junction as it approaches Churn with the 1.50pm stopping train from Oxford to Newbury on 27 February 1960.
T. B. Owen
Leica 111c 85mm Sonnar
Kodachrome 1

How different the layout at Aberystwyth looks today compared with this busy railway scene. Now almost completely devoid of sidings and reduced to one freight train per week Aberystwyth's only significant feature to remain is the locomotive shed on the left which is used to house the four 1ft 11½in gauge Vale of Rheidol engines and much of its coaching stock. The shed building seen here was a new structure built on the site of an older shed in 1938. Its GWR code was ABH and in later BR days it became a sub-shed to 89C Machynlleth, and closed to standard gauge use in April 1965. On the crisp cold morning of Christmas Eve 1962, a very dirty 'Manor' class No 7807 *Compton Manor* draws out of the goods yard with a Cambrian line goods train. *T. B. Owen*
Leica M2 50mm Summicron Kodachrome 1

A mile out of Aberystwyth the Cambrian Railway makes a short sharp 1 in 75 ascent for nearly 2 miles before dropping down to the first station (now closed) at Bow Street. In this study Collett-designed '2251' class 0-6-0 No 2260 is climbing near a hamlet called Fronfraith with the 10.25am Aberystwyth to Shrewsbury train on 16 May 1959. This locomotive was one of 120 0-6-0s built between 1930 and 1948 and was included in the first 20 constructed in 1930. In the later 1930s the class gradually superseded the earlier 'Dean Goods' and the indigenous Cambrian 0-6-0s and became regular performers over the Cambrian Railway routes. This engine was withdrawn in 1961 and only one of the class, No 3205, is preserved on the West Somerset Railway.

T. B. Owen
Leica 111c   85mm Sonnar   Kodachrome 1

Left:
A nostalgic scene at Minffordd showing '2251' class No 2232 doing some shunting in the goods yard which formed the exchange sidings with the Festiniog Railway on 29 March 1957. In the background the quarried face of Y Garth, a hill rising to 323ft, is prominent. *J. M. Jarvis Kodak Retina 1 3.5 Ektar Kodachrome 8*

Above:
A rare colour picture of a vintage GWR class of goods engine, a '2301' or 'Dean Goods' class 0-6-0 No 2538 shunting in Welshpool goods yard. Some 260 of these locomotives were built and they could be found virtually all over the GW system as their simple reliable design and modest axle loading of 11½ tons made them very useful goods engines. So much so, that in 1917, 62 were taken over by the government for the Railway Operating Division for military service in France and Greece. Most returned after World War 1 but nine did not, and two ended up in Turkey in 1919. Again on the outbreak of World War 2 another 108 were requisitioned and sold to the War Department. They went mainly to France but at least 21 were sent on to China just after the war. In 1943 six went to Tunisia whilst WD No 188 (GWR No 2435), captured by the Germans at Dunkirk in 1940, ended up in Austria in 1945 and was later claimed by the Russians! It was eventually handed back to the Austrians and scrapped in 1952. Meanwhile No 2538 seen here on 17 May 1956, had a less exciting career but nevertheless became the last survivor and was withdrawn in May 1957 from Oswestry shed. Today No 2516 remains on static display inside Swindon Railway Museum.
T. B. Owen
Leica 111c 50mm Summitar Kodachrome 8

Left:
Merthyr Tydfil High Street station is seen here on 10 September 1962, with 0-6-0PT No 6416 standing at the platform with an auto-train working to Hirwaun, a short local journey of only 7½ miles. This class of 40 engines was a Collett design fitted for auto-train working and built between 1932 and 1937. Three are preserved, two on the Dart Valley and No 6412 on the West Somerset Railway.
G. W. Morrison
Zeiss Contaflex 2.8 Tessar Agfa CT18

Above:
Overlooked by some fine semaphores, 'Hall' class No 6958 *Oxburgh Hall* stands at Newport High Street on 12 July 1960 with a short empty coaching stock working. This locomotive was one of the wartime batch of 'Halls' constructed in April 1943 and was the last of the Collett series as the succeeding engines, No 6959 onwards, featured a number of design changes introduced by Mr Hawksworth. A minor point of interest is that the 1941-44-built engines were not named as a wartime economy measure and so this engine did not receive a name until 1947. It was withdrawn in 1964.
John Edgington
Voigtlander Vito B f3.5 Skopar Agfa CT18

35

An everday scene enacted hundreds of times daily in South Wales, a typical local train of the Cardiff and Valleys area comprising a Collett '56XX' class 0-6-2T hauling a rake of non-corridor suburban coaches. No 6685, seen here on 12 July 1959, was one of 50 of the class built by contractor Sir W. G. Armstrong Whitworth in 1928. It is heading south along the quadruple-track section of line from Grangetown to Cogan Junction with a train bound for Barry Island, via Dinas Powis. In the late 19th century railways hereabouts were subject to intense competition and it was at this point the Barry Railway met the Taff Vale Railway head on, the former eventually obtaining all important running powers to get trains into Cardiff and the latter coming around the south Glamorgan coast via Penarth and Sully, to meet the Barry Railway in its heartland at Cadoxton, a suburb of Barry.

T. B. Owen
Leica 111c 85mm Sonnar Kodachrome 8

Monmouth Troy, one of two stations serving the old county town of Monmouth, was the focal point for branch lines radiating out in three directions to Ross-on-Wye, to Chepstow, and to Little Mill Junction (and thence to Pontypool Road). An auto-train comprising '14XX' class 0-4-2T No 1455 and trailer W237W is seen at Troy station on a Ross-on-Wye service. 28 May 1958. *T. B. Owen Leica 111c 50mm Summitar Kodachrome 8*

Another GWR rural focal point was the county town of Brecon where the Neath & Brecon line from Neath met the Brecon & Merthyr which served Merthyr via a joint line and Bassaleg near Newport, whilst the Cambrian and Midland Railways came from the north and east respectively by means of running powers. In this picture, looking from the east end of the station, in the distance an Ivatt Class 2 2-6-0 heads the 1.20pm to Moat Lane Junction over the Cambrian route into central Wales, a journey of 60 miles with 24 stops taking 2hr 45min, whilst 0-6-0PT No 8732 makes ready with the 12.10pm to Newport, a 47-mile journey which took only 1hr 38min! Three months later all the railways serving Brecon were closed on the orders of the infamous Richard Beeching, then the British Railways Board Chairman. 29 September 1962. *Peter A. Fry*
Kodak Retinette 1B Agfa CT18

A tranquil scene at the rural junction of Talyllyn on the former Brecon & Merthyr Railway 4 miles east of Brecon showing Collett '2251' class 0-6-0 No 3201 standing at the station with the 2.05pm train to Newport on 10 September 1962. Just behind the photographer was the junction with the Cambrian Railway with its line to Moat Lane Junction and 7¾ miles away there was another junction at Three Cocks where the Midland Railway made its connection with a line from Hereford.

G. W. Morrison

Zeiss Contaflex f2.8 Tessar Agfa CT18

An evening meet of 'Manors' at Lampeter in west Wales close by the former Cardigan and Carmarthenshire county boundaries on 1 June 1962. The 56¼-mile long secondary line from Aberystwyth to Carmarthen served sparsely populated country and in later times only had three trains each way per day. Lampeter is a small market town by the River Teifi, a noted salmon and trout river, 27½ miles from Aberystwyth so was virtually the halfway point on the line. On the left No 7815 *Fritwell Manor* stands with the 5.40pm from Aberystwyth as No 7804 *Baydon Manor* enters the station with the corresponding northbound 5.50pm from Carmarthen. Nothing now remains: the line was closed to passengers in 1965 and eventually to all traffic in 1973 whilst both the 'Manors' were withdrawn in September 1965. *Peter A. Fry Kodak Retinette 1B Agfa CT18*

On the same line as referred to opposite, 14 miles south of Aberystwyth in isolated country towards the upper reaches of the River Teifi the railway turned sharply southwards at a station called Strata Florida to follow this river for some 24 miles. There is no village of this name and the hamlet, which has the remains of a 12th century Cistercian Abbey, was 3 miles to the southeast of the station which purported to serve it! No 7815 *Fritwell Manor* stands at the station on 1 June 1962 with the 5.40pm Aberystwyth to Carmarthen train. *Peter A. Fry Kodak Retinette 1B Agfa CT18*

Above:
A historic scene at Welshpool on 6 October 1962 as Welshpool & Llanfair 2ft 6in gauge 0-6-0T No 2 *The Countess* (formerly GWR No 823 *Countess*) returns home from 6 years in store at Oswestry on a Flatrol bogie wagon, as the narrow gauge line had just been saved from demolition by the efforts of the W&L Preservation Society. Behind, looking in fine external condition, 'Manor' class No 7814 *Fringford Manor* leaves the station with the 9.45am Aberystwyth to Paddington, the up 'Cambrian Coast Express'. *Basil Roberts*
Kodak Retinette 1B Agfa CT18

Right:
Hemmed in by the Ladies Exclusive Outfitter and the Baker, 0-6-0T No 822 (ex *The Earl*) is about to edge slowly into and across Church Street, Welshpool (the main A483 road through the town), making its return journey from Llanfair Caereinion on the 2ft 6in gauge railway on 22 September 1956. Within 2 months the line was closed but thanks to the valiant efforts of a small preservation society the railway has been saved for posterity and is fully operational as a tourist line, save this section of a mile from the exchange sidings at Welshpool to the edge of the town at Raven Square. The crossing and narrow gap has now completely disappeared following road alterations in the vicinity.
John Edgington
Voigtlander Vito B f3.5 Skopar Agfa CT18

A small Cardiff Valleys division shed was situated in the high bleak moorland surroundings of Dowlais on the north eastern edge of Merthyr Tydfil at Cae Harris. This three road shed dating from 1876 was a sub-shed to Merthyr and in its latter years had a modest allocation, which by 1961 had dwindled to just three '56XX' class locomotives. This picture, taken on 19 May 1964, shows 0-6-2T No 5602, the only incumbent, standing by the coal stage with a backcloth of the hillsides upon which the railway was situated. The shed closed in December 1964.
Hugh Ballantyne
Voigtlander CLR 2.8 Skopar Agfa CT18
1/60, f5.6-8

Dowlais had no less than four stations within close proximity during the railway age and this one, Cae Harris, was the terminus of a 9½-mile long branch from Nelson & Llancaiach, jointly owned by the Great Western and Rhymney Railways. The station only had one main platform with a bay on part of its other face, and at the main platform on 19 May 1964, '56XX' class 0-6-2T No 5651 waits to leave with the 11.32am train to Ystrad Mynach. The passenger train service was withdrawn a month later. *Hugh Ballantyne*
Voigtlander CLR 2.8 Skopar Agfa CT18 1/60, f5.6

45

The crew of well groomed 'Castle' class No 5038 *Morlais Castle* wait for the right away at Kingham whilst working a short Saturday job, the 1.25pm all stations Oxford to Moreton-in-Marsh on 29 September 1962. After a pause of over 2hr the train then went forward as the 4.50pm stopping train to Worcester Shrub Hill. No 5038 was built in June 1935 and withdrawn in September 1963.
Hugh Ballantyne
Voigtlander CLR 2.8 Skopar
Perutz C18 1/60, f5.6

A Collett series '2884' class 2-8-0 No 2891 comes south through Kingham station with an up goods train heading towards Oxford on 13 April 1963. At one time Kingham was an important junction with branches west to Cheltenham and east towards Banbury with the two lines having a direct connection which crossed the main line, originally the Oxford Worcester & Wolverhampton Railway, on the black overbridge seen in the distance. Today all that·remains is the station on the main line devoid of sidings and branch lines.
Hugh Ballantyne
Voigtlander CLR 2.8 Skopar Perutz C18
1/250, f2.4-4

Above:

The Gloucester Central-Chalford auto-train service was the last survivor of a great Great Western tradition, the push-pull auto-train. This 'Chalford Flyer' service saw the inauguration in 1903 of the GWR system of auto-trains serving small conveniently placed wayside halts in country areas along the line. On 26 September 1964, with only 5 weeks to go before the suspension of service, '14XX' class 0-4-2T No 1458 leaves Gloucester with the 11.20am train to Chalford. On the right, LMS Class 8F No 48424, built to government order by the GWR at Swindon in 1943, stands outside the former GWR shed building. *Hugh Ballantyne* *Voigtlander CLR Agfa CT18 1/250, f5.6*

Right:

The preferred motive power for the 'Chalford Flyer' was the little Collett '14XX' class 0-4-2T but in later days towards the end of the steam era with many locomotives in deplorable condition, it became quite usual to see '57XX' and '94XX' class 0-6-0PTs sharing the work. Arriving at Cashes Green Halt, a mile west of Stroud on 10 October 1964, is 0-6-0PT No 9711 working the 1.08pm train from Gloucester, the third call out of 10 intermediate stops in the 16-mile journey. *Hugh Ballantyne* *Voigtlander CLR 2.8 Skopar Agfa CT18 1/250, f5.6*

By far the most important intermediate station on the Chalford route was Stroud, which is still open for Gloucester-Swindon services, 11¾ miles from Gloucester. Crossing the viaduct immediately to the west of the station 0-4-2T No 1453 approaches Stroud with the 2.10pm auto-train from Gloucester on 10 October 1964. *Hugh Ballantyne*
Voigtlander CLR 2.8 Skopar Agfa CT18
1/250, f5.6

A Sunday scene in the Cotswolds as Collett built Mogul No 7327 pulls out of Kemble on 5 August 1962 with the 1.20pm Sundays Only Paddington to Gloucester train, watched by a group of permanent way men leaning over the veranda of a Toad brake van attached to 2-8-0 No 2879, all engaged in track maintenance that afternoon. The Mogul was one of the 20 Collett variations on this Churchward designed mixed traffic engine and was built at Swindon as No 9305, renumbered in 1959 and was one of the last four class survivors being withdrawn from Didcot shed in November 1964. No 2879 like all the earlier batch of heavy goods 2-8-0s ran over a million miles during its useful life of 45 years from 1919 to 1964, and was one of the few which were never to be fitted with outside steam pipes.
Hugh Ballantyne
Voigtlander CLR 2.8 Skopar Agfa CT18
1/250, f5.6

51

The last Chief Mechanical Engineer of the GWR, Mr F. W. Hawksworth, who took office in 1941, produced one completely new tender engine design, the 'County' '1000' class two-cylinder 4-6-0 which appeared in 1945. Some features were taken from the 'Modified Hall' type but in addition the 'County' had a new Standard No 15 boiler set at 280lb/sq in pressure, coupled wheels of 6ft 3in diameter, plate frames and bogie, new pattern flat sided tender and a continuous splasher over the driving wheels. No 1000 built in August 1945 had an experimental double chimney but the subsequent 29 members of the class were constructed with single chimneys. In 1956 the boiler pressure was reduced to 250lb/sq in and a modified but short double chimney added to all the class between 1956 and 1959. This picture shows No 1018 *County of Leicester* with the modified chimney, which although detracting from the previous handsome appearance of the engine did in fact produce greater steaming efficiency. It is seen on 1 July 1962 near Rowington Junction and commencement of the four track section westwards from Lapworth with a fitted goods train heading towards Birmingham. *Michael Mensing Hasseblad 1000F 2.8 Tessar 1/1000, f3.2*

A view of a 'County' in as-built condition, except for livery. No 1026 *County of Salop* stands, very appropriately, at Shrewsbury, the county town of Shropshire, as described by the nameplate in the abbreviated form of 'Salop' on 22 September 1956. The locomotive is in spotless condition and its original chimney shows just how well the single chimney was proportioned. Also of minor interest note that the straight nameplate (an unusual feature for GWR engines) on the right side was mounted on a backing plate standing clear of the splasher, so as to allow room for the reversing lever behind it. On the left side the nameplate was affixed along the top of the splasher. No 1026 was built in January 1947, fitted with a double chimney in October 1958 and withdrawn in December 1963. *John Edgington Voigtlander Vito B f3.5 Skopar Kodachrome 8*

One of the many large Collett 2-6-2Ts of '5101' class, No 4155, at work in the West Midlands, a part of the GWR system where the class was to be found in strength for suburban passenger trains and short goods working, as seen here on 27 March 1965. No 4155 is just coming to the top of Hatton Bank, where the 1 in 110 eases on the approach to Hatton station, with a train of bricks heading towards Birmingham. This locomotive, built in 1947, was a member of a class of 140 engines dating from 1929 (and based on an earlier Churchward design) and had a short life of only 18 years, being withdrawn in July 1965. *Bryan Hicks*

In south Warwickshire '2251' class No 3217 hauls a two-coach local train in an attractive setting at Claverdon station on 1 September 1964 working as the 8.43pm Stratford-on-Avon to Leamington Spa shuttle service, a distance of only 15½ miles with a journey time of 32min, not bad for a train with five intermediate stops. This line remains open to this day and is operated by a DMU service, taking the same time for the journey. *Bryan Hicks*
Agfa Silette Agfa CT18 1/125, f5.6

Left:
A Great Western tradition was the running of Newbury race specials for members from Paddington, often 'King'-hauled direct to Newbury Racecourse station. The pride of the fleet, No 6000 *King George V*, turned out to Old Oak Common's high standard, takes special Z11 out of Paddington with one of these prestige trains in October 1962. On the right a 'Castle' makes ready to leave with a second racegoers special. *Roy Hobbs*
Agfa Silette f2.8 Solinar Kodachrome 1 1/60, f2.8

Above:
The pleasant Buckinghamshire town of Marlow is situated on the north side of the River Thames and lies at the end of a 2¾-mile long branch from Bourne End. The latter place was an intermediate station on the connecting line between Maidenhead and High Wycombe, but the section north from Bourne End has been closed and lifted so branch trains now run between Maidenhead and Marlow, reversing at Bourne End. The Marlow branch was the preserve of '14XX' class 0-4-2Ts and this is a typical train with No 1421 seen on a bright morning in August 1962 waiting to return to Bourne End. The attractive station was designed in the Italianate style which found limited use by the GWR in the period following Brunel's death in 1859 and can still be seen in the buildings at nearby Taplow. In this picture the brickwork and ornamentation is clearly visible, topped by some fine chimneys. Although the branch remains open, this lovely building has been demolished leaving just a bare platform, and all track removed save the dead-end single line.
Roy Hobbs
Agfa Silette f2.8 Solinar Kodachrome 1

Above:
The Western Region's most prestigious train was the 'Bristolian' which ran Monday to Friday nonstop Paddington to Bristol, down via Bath and up via Badminton on a limited-load 1hr 45min schedule for the 118.4 and 117.6-mile journeys respectively. On 27 May 1959, a few days before steam handed over to the D800-series diesel-hydraulics, No 6028 *King George VI* is running fast at Twyford, 31 miles from Paddington, on its westbound dash to Bristol with the 8.45am down train. *T. B. Owen*

Leica 111c 85mm Sonnar Kodachrome 8
1/200, f2.8

Right:
This picture recreates the halcyon days of Western Region steam setting the scene of a main line stopping train hauled by 'Hall' class No 5927 *Guild Hall* entering Cholsey & Moulsford station in Berkshire on 2 November 1958 with an up local train to Reading. Note the typical but prominent GWR-styled station nameboard clearly advising passengers that this was the junction for the

Wallingford branch. The short 2¾-mile long branch was closed to passengers in 1959 and general goods in 1965 but currently there is a preservation society actively seeking to reopen it. No 5927 was built in 1933 and withdrawn in 1964. The first, third and fourth non-corridor coaches in the train are still painted in the bright red livery adopted in early BR days as the standard colour for locomotive-hauled non-corridor coaching stock. *T. B. Owen*
Leica 111c 50mm Summita Kodachrome 8

CHOLSEY AND MOULSFORD
CHANCE FOR WALLINGFORD

Deadweight on the drawbar for one of Mr Collett's heavy goods Class 7200 2-8-2Ts No 7221 on a cold day towards the end of winter as it slogs upgrade towards Patchway station at the top of an unremitting hard climb from the bottom of the Severn Tunnel with nearly seven miles of almost continuous 1 in 100 against the load of 18 24ton Dogfish loaded ballast wagons and Shark brake van. This locomotive was one of 54 rebuilds from earlier 2-8-0Ts having been rebuilt from No 5256 in 1935. It was withdrawn in November 1964 but three of the class have been preserved, although at the time of publication none are in operational service. 17 March 1962. *Hugh Ballantyne*
Voigtlander CLR 2.8 Skopar Perutz C18 f5.6 1/250

Pale winter sunlight on Christmas Eve 1962 shines on Churchward Mogul '43XX' class No 6304 which had just arrived at Gloucester Central, with steam to spare, on the 10.25am train from Hereford. The '43s' had good route availability so could be found over much of the Great Western system including extensive use from Gloucester shed on the Hereford trains. No 6304 was built in 1920, fitted with outside steam pipes in 1952 and withdrawn in January 1964. *Peter A. Fry*
Kodak Retinette 1B   Agfa CT18

Until BR rationalisation there were four tracks on the six route miles between Gloucester and Cheltenham Lansdown, the Great Western and the Midland originally having their separate, but parallel, double lines. On this busy section 'Modified Hall' '6959' class No 6969 *Wraysbury Hall* heads towards Gloucester on 16 May 1964 with a long fitted goods train. *Hugh Ballantyne Voigtlander CLR 2.8 Skopar Agfa CT18 1/250, f5.6*

Not long after its last overhaul at Swindon Gloucester's '5101' class 2-6-2T No 4107 is seen on 20 July 1963 approaching Standish Junction on the GWR line to Swindon with a mixed goods train, much of which comprises army lorries on flat wagons. At this point there was a junction between the Great Western and Midland lines before the routes changed direction, the Western ran to Stroud and Swindon, and the Midland continued due south to Mangotsfield and Bristol. Note in the bottom left corner of the picture the Midland Railway milepost 100, the distance being measured from Derby. *Hugh Ballantyne*
Voigtlander CLR 2.8 Skopar Agfa CT18
1/125, f4

Left:
Tank engines under repair in A Shop at Swindon Works. Right until the end of steam Swindon maintained its tradition of quality repairs and its impeccable turn out of locomotives which was unsurpassed by any other railway workshops. Engines receiving attention in this picture taken on 28 July 1963 are 0-6-0PT No 9663 and 2-6-2T No 4115. *Hugh Ballantyne*
Voigtlander CLR 2.8 Skopar Agfa CT18 1/15, f4

Above:
On the north side of the huge Swindon complex was the Stock Shed used mainly for storage and latterly the sidings holding engines awaiting withdrawal or scrapping. When this picture was taken of 'County' class No 1013 *County of Dorset* on 20 September 1964, it had been withdrawn 2 months, hence its sad appearance bereft of name, number plates and connecting rods. The Dynamometer Car No W7W was built at Swindon in 1901 and used for road testing locomotives to measure their effectiveness as power units. The vehicle has a distinctive clerestory roof and a bodyside bulge amidships for observation purposes. Inside it has a saloon for the instruments and a Hallade recorder for recording speeds which was operated by the large flangeless retractable wheel visible near the bogie. This coach was used in the famous Locomotive Exchanges of 1948 but when a replacement dynamometer car was built in 1961 it was retired. It is seen here stored out of use when the intention was to scrap it, but fortuitously it was subsequently saved for preservation and is now at Buckfastleigh on the Dart Valley Railway.
Hugh Ballantyne
Voigtlander CLR 2.8 Skopar Agfa CT18 1/60, f8-11

On page 64 reference was made to the high standard of repairs to locomotives at Swindon and the pictures on this and the opposite page are included for you to see in colour just how good that standard was. Of course Swindon men swore that engines received for repair by them were in fact in better condition on arrival than many despatched ex-works from railway workshops in other parts of the country! The scene above on 15 April 1962 was a familiar sight outside the entrance to the enormous A Shop where engines stood parked prior to having their tenders attached and then weighed before going out on running-in trials (see pages 18 and 24). 'Hall' class No 5978 *Bodinnick Hall* is buffered up to 'Castle' class No 5026 *Criccieth Castle*, one of the class fitted with a double chimney. Almost certainly this was the last major repair for both locomotives as No 5978 was withdrawn in October 1963 and No 5026 in November 1964.

T. B. Owen

Leica M2 35mm Summicron Kodachrome 1

On the right is one of the 10 'Manor' class light 4-6-0s built after the war No 7824 *Iford Manor* in impeccable condition ready for running in trials before return to its home shed at Carmarthen. No 7824 had a short life, being constructed in December 1950 and withdrawn in November 1964. It was seen at Swindon on 4 May 1958. *T. B. Owen Leica 111c 50mm Summitar Kodachrome 8*

This 1957 scene at Birmingham Snow Hill station shows a 'Hall' class No 5967 *Bickmarsh Hall* looking very clean and tidy with an unidentified '28XX' class 2-8-0 standing behind. Both light engines are on the up line through the station, possibly on their way to Tyseley shed for servicing. *John Edgington Voigtlander Vito B f3.5 Skopar Kodachrome 8*

An unidentified 'King' class 4-6-0 approaches
Birmingham Snow Hill station with the 8.50am
from Birkenhead Woodside to Paddington express
in April 1962. *John Edgington*
Voigtlander Vito B f3.5 Skopar Afga CT18

15

An interesting view at Worcester looking north in the direction of Rainbow Hill Tunnel taken from a vantage point between the loco shed building out of sight on the left and the locomotive, carriage and wagon works building partly visible on the right. On 1 June 1963 'Hall' class No 4905 *Barton Hall*, one of the first of the class to be constructed in 1928, brings an up goods on the approach towards Shrub Hill station passing BR Standard Class 4 4-6-0 No 75005 and a line of unfitted wagons containing locomotive coal. *R. C. Riley*
Agfa Super Silette f2 Solagon Kodachrome 1

Portrait of a distinguished member of Mr Collett's 'Castle' class No 5054 *Earl of Ducie* standing at Worcester Shrub Hill station on 12 July 1964, waiting to depart to South Wales with an enthusiasts special from Derby which had arrived behind an 'A1' class Pacific No 60114 *W. P. Allen*. Despite the fact this engine was in fine fettle when photographed it was withdrawn from service 3 months later whilst only 2 months previously it had been one of the especially selected three 'Castles' involved in a high speed triangular journey Paddington-Plymouth-Bristol-Paddington organised by Ian Allan Ltd to commemorate the 60th anniversary of the 'Ocean Mail' run by *City of Truro*. The Western Region rose to the occasion magnificently on 9 May 1964 providing No 4079 *Pendennis Castle* on the first leg which unfortunately failed near Westbury and was replaced by No 6999 *Capel Dewi Hall* to Taunton and No 7025 *Sudeley Castle* to Plymouth. The return to Bristol had No 7029 *Clun Castle*, and this engine was chosen for the last high speed gallop to Paddington via Badminton on 'Bristolian' timings. *Earl of Ducie* with its 265 tons load ran the 117.6 miles in 95min 33sec against the booked time of 100min, giving a start to stop average speed of 73.8mph. The author will never forget the thrilling sound — like the roar of a motorcycle engine working flat out — when No 5054 swept past at the anticipated fastest point of its journey where the line crosses the River Avon near Little Somerford at the bottom of a 9-mile descent at 1 in 300, at what was later calculated to be 94mph. This was truly a grand finale for these fine locomotives. No 5054 was built in June 1936 as *Lamphey Castle* and renamed *Earl of Ducie* in September 1937, one of 21 'Castles' to be named after Earls of the realm, and names which had originally been allocated to 4-4-0s of the '32XX' class. *Hugh Ballantyne*

Voigtlander CLR 2.8 Skopar Afga CT18 1/60, f5.6

In south Somerset the branch between Yeovil and Taunton had originated in 1853 as a Bristol & Exeter Railway broad gauge branch from Durston Junction to Yeovil Hendford and then extended to Yeovil Pen Mill in 1857. In 1906 the section west of Langport became part of the GWR shortened main line to the west of England with the opening of the cut-off via Somerton to Castle Cary. This picture taken at Hendford, on the west side of Yeovil shows the station only had a single platform but there was a goods yard to the east side of the station. Despite transfer to Southern Region jurisdiction, (the reason for the Great Western signalbox being painted in Southern Region colours) Western engines were the usual mainstay of branch trains with '45XX' class 2-6-2Ts predominating, although BR Standards and Southern engines did appear from time to time. 'Prairie' No 4593 is seen entering the platform with the 2.10pm Taunton to Yeovil Pen Mill train on 13 June 1964, the last day of service. Behind is part of the Westland aircraft factory complex. The branch was closed from 15 June 1964 and No 4593 withdrawn 3 months later.

Hugh Ballantyne
Voigtlander CLR 2.8 Skopar Agfa CT18
1/250, f4

Bruton, a small town in south Somerset, is situated on the West of England main line from Reading to Taunton via Westbury, but originally was a station on the Wilts, Somerset & Weymouth Railway which was opened as far as Yeovil in 1856 and extended to Weymouth the following year. Although the opening of the Castle Cary-Durston-Cogload Junction cut-off line in June 1906 made this railway part of the new main line, trains serving the station today are those working the Bristol-Weymouth cross country service. The town retains its station but it is now reduced to an unstaffed halt. In more prosperous times 'Hall' class No 6955 *Lydcott Hall* has climbed the 1 in 98 rise into the station from Castle Cary with the 8.57am Weymouth Town to Newbury semi-fast on 18 August 1962.
Peter A. Fry
Kodak Retinette 1B   Agfa CT18

73

Running along the southern escarpment of the Mendip Hills is a series of small and very attractive market towns, Shepton Mallet, Wells and Cheddar. These places were served by the GWR (and Wells by the Somerset & Dorset from Glastonbury) from Yatton to Witham, a distance of 31¾ miles. The Bristol & Exeter (B&E) line from Yatton reached Wells in 1870 and was known as the Cheddar Valley branch whilst the railway coming from Witham was opened in 1862 as the East Somerset Railway. Originally Wells had no less than three stations all within a radius of a third of a mile, and in 1878 the B&E station shown here, called Tucker Street, was brought into use for through train running. Wells was the focal point of train services with an average of seven from the Yatton direction against four to and from Witham. Eventually the Beeching 'Axe' fell on the whole branch and on the last day of operation, 7 September 1963, the fireman on Collett 0-6-0 No 3218 hands to the signalman the staff of the final 2.45pm Yatton to Witham and Frome train.

Hugh Ballantyne
Voigtlander CLR 2.8 Skopar Agfa CT18
1/125, f5.6

Bristol Bath Road shed's small allocation of Ivatt designed Class 2 2-6-2Ts found regular work on the Cheddar Valley/East Somerset line, and here No 41245 leaves the attractive Cheddar station on 17 August 1963 with the 3.28pm Witham to Yatton train. The photograph clearly shows some B&E features of the station, local Mendip stone construction with overall roof, decorative barge boards a roof of tiles with alternating bands of plain and pattern tiles and, not least, twisted terracotta chimney pots, altogether adding up to an architectural gem of a station. *Hugh Ballantyne Voigtlander CLR 2.8 Skopar Agfa CT18 1/125, f5.6*

Under a threatening sky double-chimnyed 'Castle' class No 5060 *Earl of Berkeley* is running well and with steam to spare past Oldfield Park and Westmoreland Road goods yard at Bath with the Saturdays Only 10.35am Weston-super-Mare to Paddington express on 21 July 1962. By the time this photograph was taken in the summer of 1962 virtually all the Paddington-Bristol turns were diesel-hydraulic hauled and it was only on Saturdays when the 'Kings' and 'Castles' were seen in the area on their old top link jobs. 21 July 1962.
Hugh Ballantyne
Voigtlander CLR 2.8 Skopar Agfa CT18
1/250, f5.6

Not quite what it appears as 'Castle' class No 5015 *Kingswear Castle* heads westwards out of Bath past Westmoreland Road goods yard with the Saturdays Only down 8.45am Paddington to Weston-super-Mare on 21 July 1962, incorrectly proclaimed to be the 'Bristolian'. On Mondays to Fridays the 8.45am down was the 'Bristolian' nonstop to Bristol, but on Saturdays the load was strengthened from seven to 11 or 12 coaches, a stop at Bath was added and the train continued on to Weston-super-Mare. In the penultimate summer of main line steam working on the Bristol road, Old Oak Common shed staff would sometimes put the headboard on the front of the engine of the Saturday train unofficially as a pleasant reminder of the great steam days past. No 5015 was built in 1932 and withdrawn in April 1963. *Hugh Ballantyne*
Voigtlander CLR 2.8 Skopar Agfa CT18 1/250, f4

Above:
An interesting picture taken in November 1964 on the Cambrian Railway main line between Whitchurch and Welshpool showing Arddleen Halt, situated on the section of line between the River Vyrnwy and River Severn and 9¼ miles from Oswestry. Lightweight 'Manor' class 4-6-0 No 7819 *Hinton Manor* is passing the halt, nonstop, with a local train from Oswestry to Welshpool. This locomotive, built at Swindon in 1939 and withdrawn in 1965, is perhaps today one of the best known preserved GWR engines, having been restored on the Severn Valley Railway and returned to service in 1977, where it not only performs a great deal of

work but has also travelled extensively on the Western Region during GW150 Year in 1985 and back on Cambrian Coast runs during the summer of 1987. This section of the Cambrian lost its passenger train service on 18 January 1965. *Roy Hobbs*
Agfa Silette f2.8 Solinar Kodachrome II
1/250, f2.8

Right:
At the inland resort of Dolgellau, situated in a fold in the mountains to the north of Cader Idris, this picture recalls the past era of the railway age and the country train as part of the every day scene, showing Collett '2251' class 0-6-0 No 2276

approaching Dolgellau station on 18 August 1962 with the 11.30am train from Pwllheli to Ruabon. The station was situated just to the north of the town on the north bank of the River Wnion, and today the location has changed out of all recognition with a new carriageway for the A487 road having completely obliterated all traces of the station and evidence of the track formation. This long secondary line of 53 miles between Ruabon and Barmouth Junction was closed to passenger traffic on 18 January 1965. *Peter W. Gray*
Agfa Super Silette Kodachrome 1

Left:
Bird's eye view of Taffs Well Junction looking northwards up the valley of the River Taff towards Pontypridd. This picture was taken on 13 May 1965 from the mighty Walnut Tree Viaduct — 1,548ft long — which soared across the Nantgarw Gap 120ft above the Taff Vale and Cardiff Railways, and carried the Barry Railway towards Penrhos Junction and its vital connection with the Rhymney Railway, and the vast coal traffic that this route generated — no less than 1½ million tons per annum in 1904. In this scene '56XX' class 0-6-2T No 5692 is banking a coal train hauled by D6975

past Taffs Well station on the quadruple track main line on the TVR. To the right a train is coming off the former Rhymney Railway connection from Caerphilly to the TVR, as this location was a focal point for no less than four GWR constituent companies, the Taff Vale, Barry, Rhymney and Cardiff Railway. *Hugh Ballantyne*
Voigtlander CLR 2.8 Skopar Agfa CT18
1/125, f8

Above:
Deep in the valley of the River Ebbw just south of Abertillery was a junction and extensive sidings at

Aberbeeg. Here the lines to Brynmawr and Ebbw Vale bifurcated and in view of the amount of goods traffic generated there was a four-road locomotive shed opened in 1911, which had a fleet of about 35 engines, mainly '57XX' class 0-6-0PTs. In this photograph three pannier tanks are visible with No 4688 en route to Ebbw Vale on 19 April 1962.
T. B. Owen
Leica M2 50mm Summicron Kodachrome 1

Left:

No book portraying the lines of the Great Western Railway would be complete without illustrating one of the company's best remembered features and not found on any other railway system. This was the standard 'Type A' shelter designed for use on lineside halts and platforms which were developed in the 1900s with the introduction of rail motor services. These distinctive waiting shelters, clad with corrugated galvanised sheeting, quickly became known as 'Pagodas'. Approaching Cove Halt, on the Exe Valley branch between Bampton and Tiverton, is '14XX' class 0-4-2T No 1450 with an afternoon working from Exeter to Dulverton on

15 June 1963. The halt was installed in March 1923; previously from the opening of the railway in 1884 there had only been a goods siding here, and throughout the remaining life of the branch until its closure on 5 October 1963 Cove was the only place on the line to have a Pagoda. No 1450 has been more fortunate; following withdrawal in 1965 it was sold in running order and can now be seen working in Devon on the Dart Valley Railway.
L. F. Folkard
Agfa Silette Kodachrome I

Above:
Further south on the Exe Valley branch 0-4-2T

No 1421 pulls out of Cadeleigh station on 28 September 1963 with the 1.45pm train from Tiverton to Exeter. This station was situated in a picturesque setting close by the village of Bickleigh and originally when opened in 1885, it was more correctly named Cadeleigh & Bickleigh, as Cadeleigh is some 1½ miles up a steep hill to the northwest. The name was shortened to Cadeleigh in 1906 to avoid confusion with the Bickleigh station on the Plym Valley branch. *Hugh Ballantyne*
Voigtlander CLR 2.8 Skopar Agfa CT18
1/125, f8

The '61XX' class 2-6-2Ts were built for London area suburban services and had a higher boiler pressure of 225lb/sq in against the 200lb/sq in of their almost identical cousins the '5101' class, and this increased their power for the demanding job of fast acceleration between numerous stops on London area local services. Although allocated to most London Division sheds the greatest numbers worked from Old Oak Common, Southall, Slough and Reading. This engine, No 6165, was a Reading locomotive for many years but when photographed in 1963 painted in unlined green livery it was employed on an ECS working at Old Oak Common. It was constructed in 1935 and lasted until the very end in December 1965, then subsequently sold to J. Cashmore Ltd of Newport for scrap. 19 October 1963. *T. B. Owen Leica M2 85mm Sonnar Kodachrome 1*

The neat compact lines of the little Collett designed '14XX' class 0-4-2T is evident in this study of No 1466 standing in the down bay platform at Exeter St David's on 22 June 1962, waiting to leave with a branch train to Tiverton. The engine is painted in unlined black livery with the original BR emblem on the tank side. Built in 1936 and withdrawn in 1963 this is one of four out of a class of 75 of these push-pull fitted engines to be preserved. It is owned and kept by the Great Western Society at its depot at Didcot in working order.
K. Falconer
Voigtlander Vito B   Kodachrome 1

The classic coastal section of line between Dawlish and Teignmouth was understandably much favoured by the publicity conscious GWR as a backcloth for many of its publicity pictures. On a fine summer afternoon in September 1955 'Castle' class No 7011 *Banbury Castle* passes the down Teignmouth distant signal with the 'Torbay Express', the 12.30pm from Paddington to Kingswear, in a setting of the azure blue of the English Channel and the red sandstone cliffs of the South Devon coast hereabouts, a colourful setting in one of England's loveliest counties. *J. M. Jarvis*
Kodak Retina 1 3.5 Ektar Kodachrome 8

As it is quite early in the summer season and outside school holidays, the beach at Dawlish has plenty of space for everyone as 'Castle' class No 5017 *The Gloucestershire Regiment 28th, 61st* heads up the coast towards Dawlish Warren with the 11.12am Kingswear to Paddington — the up 'Torbay Express' — on 16 June 1958 with a neat set of Mk 1 stock painted in the then recently re-introduced chocolate and cream livery which the Western Region was allocating to its best named express trains. No 5017 was originally named *St Donats Castle* when built in 1932 but was renamed in April 1954 to commemorate the Regiment's gallant campaign in the Korean War. It was withdrawn from service in July 1962. *T. B. Owen*
Leica 111c 85mm Sonnar
Kodachrome 8

The first of the 'Grange' class 4-6-0s No 6800 *Arlington Grange's* sharp bark reverberates against the hillside as it pounds up the 1 in 41 gradient past Stoneycombe Sidings towards Dainton Tunnel with a Penzance train on 14 June 1958. This locomotive was built in 1936 and withdrawn in June 1964: none of the class of 80 engines having been preserved.
T. B. Owen
Leica 111c   85mm Sonnar   Kodachrome 8

The largest and smallest of the GWR 4-6-0 types combine to haul an up Penzance to Paddington express over the formidable section of railway between Plymouth and Newton Abbot, noted for its succession of sharp curves and very steep gradients. Up trains from Plymouth faced 2 miles of 1 in 42 from Plympton up Hemerdon Bank, and here on 14 June 1958 'Manor' class No 7809 *Childrey Manor* is piloting 'King' class No 6013 *King Henry VIII* as they slowly pass the Hemerdon distant signal towards a welcome easing of the gradient.

T. B. Owen

Leica 111c 85mm Sonnar Kodachrome 8

When this picture was taken as long ago as 1961 the diesel-hydraulics had captured almost complete control of Western Region trains in the Plymouth area, but one regular steam turn through 1961 was the 11.20am Plymouth to Taunton local train. On 7 August 1961, a well cleaned 'Hall' class No 6946 *Heatherden Hall* passes the small signalbox at Dainton (later replaced by a more modern but less imposing structure on the same site) at the top of a 1 in 43 climb before entering Dainton Tunnel, which would be followed by the downhill run to Aller Junction and the next stop at Newton Abbot.

Hugh Ballantyne
Voigtlander CLR 2.8 Skopar Agfa CT18
1/250, f5.6

A broad gauge branch line was opened from Marsh Mills, Tavistock Junction, to Tavistock in 1859 by the South Devon Railway and 6 years later extended over the county boundary to Launceston in Cornwall, a distance of 32 miles. The principal intermediate station was at Tavistock, an attractive market town to the west of Dartmoor which boasted two stations, as it was also served by the LSWR line from Plymouth to Okehampton and Exeter. This is a view of the GWR station, by then known as Tavistock South, looking towards Plymouth and showing '4575' class 2-6-2T No 5572 standing at the platform after arrival with the 1.25pm from Saltash on 8 August 1961. This engine is now owned by the Great Western Society and kept in working order at Didcot. The branch closed to all traffic on 29 December 1962, a day in which the weather deteriorated to a severe blizzard by the evening of the last train and heralded the start of the great winter freeze of 1962/63. *Hugh Ballantyne Voigtlander CLR 2.8 Skopar Agfa CT18 1/60, f4*

After the long-serving LSWR Beattie 2-4-0WTs had been withdrawn from Wadebridge shed in 1961, the china clay branch trains to Wenford Bridge had three of the six Collett '1366' class 0-6-0PTs as replacements until dieselisation in 1964. The neat and compact lines of No 1368 are evident in this picture as it brings a load of china clay off the Wenford Bridge line at Dunmere Junction on 4 May 1964. *Roy Hobbs*
Agfa Silette 2.8 Solinar Kodachrome II

How different the railway scene is today with its unkempt, often unstaffed, stations devoid of even basic facilities, surrounded by litter and uncontrolled lineside vegetation and undergrowth, compared with this scene of a well maintained railway infrastructure and the neat tracksides. On 14 September 1958 2-6-2T No 4587 draws out of Shepherds station with the 9.12am train from Newquay to Truro. This branch, which left the main line to Penzance at Chacewater ran to Newquay via Perranporth, a distance of 18¾ miles, was closed from 4 February 1963. *T. B. Owen*
Leica 111c 85mm Sonnar
Kodachrome 8

Left:
Two pictures to show the end of Great Western steam on the Western Region. On Friday 11 June 1965 the last scheduled passenger train to be steam hauled was the 16.15 departure from Platform 3 at Paddington to Banbury, seen here hauled by No 7029 *Clun Castle.* *Hugh Ballantyne Voigtlander CLR 2.8 Skopar Agfa CT18 1/60, f8*

Above:
The official Western Region 'Last Steam Special' from Paddington on 27 November 1965 was also hauled by No 7029 *Clun Castle* and appropriately ran down Mr Brunel's main line of railway to Bristol via Bath, then travelled northwards to Gloucester via the Midland route out of Bristol, before retracing its steps back to Paddington via Swindon.

The late autumn sunshine appears just at the right moment as *Clun Castle* traverses the 'foreign' metals of the Midland Railway at Mangotsfield as it heads towards Gloucester. *Hugh Ballantyne Voigtlander CLR 2.8 Skopar Agfa CT18 1/250, f4*

Above:
To conclude this look at the Great Western scene in colour. I include this extremely rare colour picture of one of a small class of three which were the last survivors of a total of 29 locomotives taken over from the Midland & South Western Junction Railway by the GWR on 1 July 1923. This trio of delightful little 2-4-0s pottered about in the Reading and Didcot area for many years, often to be seen gently meandering up and down the Newbury to Lambourn branch. All three, GWR numbers 1334 to 1336 were built by Dubs & Co in 1894. This engine, No 1336, was the last survivor of the trio and is leaving Cirencester Watermoor with a Gloucestershire Railway Society special over part of its home railway on 9 May 1953. Less than a year later, in March 1954, it too was withdrawn.
J. M. Jarvis
Kodak Retina 1 3.5 Ektar Kodachrome 8 1/100, f4

Back cover:
In many places Western Region sheds endeavoured to maintain the tradition of the old GWR of gleaming engines and polished brass. Right up to the 1960s Canton, the principal Cardiff shed, kept its passenger locomotives in good condition and this is a typical example of the era with the evening sun catching the Brunswick green paintwork, brass and copper of No 5903 *Keele Hall* crossing the River Avon into Bath Spa station on 28 August 1961 with the 5.25pm Salisbury to Cardiff train.
Hugh Ballantyne
Voigtlander CLR Agfa CT18 1/250, f4